MOOSE

Michio Hoshino

Chronicle Books · San Francisco

Acknowledgments

I am deeply indebted to the following people for their
interest and support of this publication:

Karen Colligan-Taylor
Eliza Jones
People in Huslia
University of Alaska: Alaska Native Language Center
Denali National Park

First published in the United States 1988 by
Chronicle Books.
Copyright © 1988 by Michio Hoshino.
All rights reserved. No part of this book may be reproduced in
any form without written permission from Chronicle Books.
Printed in Japan.
First published in Japan by Heibonsha, Publisher, Tokyo.
Library of Congress Cataloging-in-Publication Data
Hoshino, Michio, 1952–
    Moose.

    1. Moose.   I. Title.
QL737.U53H67   1988   599.73'57   88-11466
ISBN 0-87701-494-9 (pbk.)
ISBN 0-87701-503-1

Translated by Karen Colligan-Taylor.

Distributed in Canada by
Raincoast Books
112 East 3rd Avenue
Vancouver, B.C.
V5T 1C8
10 9 8 7 6 5 4 3

Chronicle Books
275 Fifth Street
San Francisco, California 94103

DINEEGA

A translation of this text, which is printed in the Athapaskan language, appears on the next page.

Yagga eey go an kk'oheedidaał tuh yagga k'ahalaayh hu eey go dineega go bilił daalitł'idzee gin eey hay'alaaya ghoyinee-haghaalneek ahu tłeedohuditodliliyhdlaa, go yagga k'ildlaaninh koon yagga donła' hoozoonh ts'a bakk'ohoonotłtok duhughunh. Ginee eey kk'udaa ts'iłonaayee yagga yoogh dineega dzotin lił yił dineega tłeetł lił yił hałda ts'itł ghaats'aghadeelaayh. Yagga huts'inh bits'ildlaanh hu tł'ee bahootolaa' duhughunh.

Eey go kk'o' hoołdlaa'aa don hałda hugh nohuhulnik eey go sinaatłyon kkaa. Eet hałda k'uhgaal yuh dinaalo' aahaa ts'eetołkil yaan' aghadilaak. Go gguh koonh yagga diyh koonh tł'ogho hunonłts'a hoogheelaa', dilbagga koonh. Go bidziyh hałda tł'eeltin' aahaa huyaan'. Tł'ogho eey nił dint'aan kkaa yaan' k'a'alaayh. Ts'uh eey go k'a'alaayinh hałda hutł'ok'ilkik. Uhts'a tł'ee duhut'aanh huldon' tuh eey go dineega gho nohoodileet tuh dineega a'alaayinh yagga tł'ee k'a'ałdlaaghaay kkaa tł'ok'iłkik, yagga bilił daalitł'idza koonh. Hulookk'ut koon yagga tłaahu diyee k'iłdoyinh dibaa'een ditłiga tł'ok'iłkik. Saakkaay deegudzaay kkaa yagga tłaahu hay'alaay neełot don ghadahdla kkaa tł'aahałkik. Go at'aghłdoo' nooyoogh neełyił daadlitł'ee eeneen' kkáa tł'ee uhudahat'aanh yooghadon dahot'eek ts'in'. Yagga donta' hoozoonhts'a habakk'ohoonołtok duhughunh.

Eey go dinaak'a kk'adonts'idnee' kk'aatugh hał yagga yoogh dibaa da'aneeyh tuh no'oogh huts'uhu habaahaa hool'onh. Ts'uhu yoogh'aay'oogha lidoninh akk'ots'inaałtoyh kk'a habits'oodaadakkoyh. Yagga baaba tłinozilyaayh hałda yagga kk'adonts'idnee kk'aatugha. Yagga habiyił neehudah da hałda k'eelugh dinaabaaba anaahadlinaghaa. Ts'uh habits'oodaadakkoyh. Ts'uh kkudaa yoogh nohudilik ts'uh kk'udaa habakk'aa too neelk'uh. Go too eenolk'uhtł ta hałda yoogh baaba zoo' ditłiga kk'ał neeliyaayh. Yoogh dineega tłee' yił. Ts'uh yagga kk'odaadlakkon dittiga yagga ees habiyeeya'. Ts'uh yagga kk'odaadlakkon hałda yee neełghanohoditł'ooł go kk'adonts'idnee kk'aatugha.

Catherine Attla

DINEEGA (MOOSE)

People have to take good care of the game they get, such as moose or bear. If they don't, game will become scarce and hunters will have bad luck. When we get a moose, we hang up on willows or trees the parts we're not going to bring home, such as the skin of the moose head and the leg skins. We do this to show respect, so the spirit of the animal will return to the land.

Life was hard long ago because hunting was done on foot with bows and arrows and spears. My grandparents used to say that they had to get nearly everything they killed by hand. They also had to be good runners. In the winter if people wanted to go fast or far, they would use a dog team. In the summer they would row a boat or pull it by rope. Moose were scarce then, so they went a long way to hunt them. In my earliest memory there were no moose. We started seeing moose in the 1930s, but even in the 1950s there still weren't many.

The successful hunters always shared food. It has always been important to share, and we still practice it today. When the moose season opens and hunters get a moose, they give some meat to those who haven't killed a moose yet. We do the same thing with bear and fish. When a child catches fish or game for the first time, he shares it with an elderly person for good luck.

Sometimes people call on Raven for help. One of the things we say to Raven while we hunt is "Tseek'aał, sits'a nohaałtee'oyh," which means "Grandpa, drop a pack to me." If the bird caws and rolls, it is a sign of good luck. Raven is protected because it is said that he helped shape the world. That is why the one who raised me used to tell more Raven stories than any others. He was a medicine man and he was familiar with Raven power. People also talk to Raven when they see it out in the woods, especially when they are alone. They talk to Raven the same way we pray to God. Besides talking to Raven, people pray to Bit'ohɨdeełt'aa. I don't know what Bit'ohɨdeełt'aa is. It must be God. It means "that which we depend on for life."

We have potlatch because, according to our stories, when people die they don't leave right away. They stay nearby and they don't forget our food. So we burn food for them to eat. At first we burn food every day, then every other day, then once a week, and so on. Then, after a year, we make a memorial potlatch. We serve the best food we have at the potlatch, because for the last time we are feeding the person who died. We serve foods like moose head soup, because that's not something we eat every day. It is special.

We depend on fish and game for subsistence. If we don't take care of the land and the game, it will become scarce and we will have a hard time. It will be the same as for the person who depends on money but doesn't have it.

Michio's work will give the public a better understanding of our relationship with land and animals and of how we depend on them. When Michio came, he didn't have a gun to hunt with, only a camera. Although he went on a hunting trip with us last year and this year, he never shot a moose; he just took pictures. He also helped us by handling meat for us when we had luck. He's like a son to us.

Catherine Attla

INTRODUCTION

Michio first came to see me at my home in Moose, Wyoming. Appropriately enough, he was planning a photo book about moose! As we had tea by my fireplace while a fierce snowstorm howled outside, I was impressed by this young man's enthusiasm and devotion to learning about animals. I wondered a bit, however, about his patience—his ability to sit or stand, and wait and watch and closely observe, as I had done so many times with my naturalist husband, Olaus. But now we have Michio's book *Grizzly*, and there is no question about his patience!

I would like, here and now, to clear up, if I can, the confusion about the name of the animal we in America call moose. The name *elch* in German (*elg* in Norwegian) is the European name for the animal we here call moose. How the animal the American natives called *wapiti* came to be called "elk" is an unsolved mystery. In New Zealand, where elk (*wapiti*) from Jackson Hole, Wyoming, were introduced in 1905, they are never called anything but wapiti. As for the name moose, that is the native American name for the *elg* of Norway.

I have been reading *The Moose Book* by Samuel Merrill, published in 1916, in which he quotes from one of the earliest explorers of New England, William Wood, who wrote in 1634:

"The beast called a Moose, is not much unlike red deare; this beast is as bigge as an Oxe; slow of foot, headed like a Bucke, with a broade beame, some being two yards wide in the head; their flesh is as good as Beefe, their hides good for cloathing."

From this 1634 description of a moose (with 1634 spellings), it would seem that the animal has changed very little. But the history of the moose began in Asia a million years ago; the moose was alive and well while the mammoth still roamed the north country. Mr. Merrill also quotes Henry Fairfield Osborn, who wrote in the early 1900s: "Nature has been a million years in developing that wonderful animal, and man should not ruthlessly destroy it."

Only a little research reveals that the moose has had, during those million years, more legend and myth circulated about it, and probably more use made of its entire anatomy, from the tiny bone in its heart, thought to be of medicinal value, to its left hind hoof, for the same reason, than any other animal.

Traveling with Olaus, I have watched moose in many parts of Alaska—at the Kenai, the Koyukuk, the Yukon, the Porcupine, and the Sheenjek—and in British Columbia and Wyoming. We know there are still many in New England and thousands in Sweden —it is truly a circumpolar animal.

At Moose, where I live, we meet and watch eight or nine of them at all seasons—safe in a national park. There is a special indescribable thrill and satisfaction in just knowing that they are there, in the forest, on the meadow, in the beaver pond, tolerating us. Man, so far, has not destroyed.

Michio has spent more than eight years following and photographing the animals of Alaska. The results are most impressive. They are a joy to gaze at, and they bring a message to all who see them.

Michio is now back in Alaska where there is a wealth of wildlife for him to watch and study and photograph. His message continues clear: "Nature deserves care; wild creatures and their habitats enrich our lives."

We can pray that man will not "ruthlessly destroy" any of them and that the moose may quietly pursue its ways in the forests for a long, long time.

Margaret E. Murie

A cow and two moose calves drink water while resting in a tundra filled with
autumn colors. Denali (Mount McKinley) rises in the distance.

A bull moose in rut wanders about Naknek Lake in search of a cow.

A moose lingers in newly fallen snow. In the distance is the snow-capped Alaska Range.

This largest member of the deer family is taller than a thoroughbred and weighs more than a cow.

THE ALASKAN MOOSE

Suddenly the old woman began to sing in a low, monotonous voice.

All of the villagers had gathered in a log cabin, where they formed a large circle. In the center of the circle were the old woman and the family of the deceased. There was strength in that flat rhythm. It was the kind of song that would echo through the depths of one's heart. The family members at the center closed their eyes and began to dance slowly to the rhythm of the song. As the only outsider at this gathering, I stood back in a corner absorbing the scene before me. At some point the circle formed by the villagers had begun to rotate slowly.

One year had passed since the death of an old woman in the village. Today there was a potlatch. This was a banquet held to dispatch the spirit of the dead. Today the soul would begin its journey.

The table was set with the meat of black bear and beaver, salmon, blueberries and cranberries — the soul would be dispatched with a feast from nature. I had just returned from a moose-hunting trip with one of the village families. The meat from that moose and soup made from its head were also being served. Moose head soup, made by boiling and completely dissolving the head, was a dish that could not be omitted from this banquet. For the Athapaskan Indians of this region, moose provided the "sacred food" of the potlatch.

People danced and ate and spoke of the deceased. The atmosphere within the cabin had attained a fervor that transformed sorrow over death into a mysterious lightheartedness. Nature breathed around the cabin. Just beyond its walls stretched the forest. What were the boundaries of this forest and the river that ran through it? The river along which we had sought the moose was now flowing into the depths of night. As I watched the dance become more animated, I thought about the wilderness that surrounds the daily life of these people, and about the beliefs of a people who live at the hand of nature. I recalled the days of the hunt just completed.

"*Dineega* is our Indian word for moose," explained Catherine as she added another branch to the fire. Sparks rose into the air, together with

An Athapaskan Indian girl.

the fragrance of spruce resin.

"In the past, every year at the onset of autumn, we would leave the village and set out on a long hunting trip. We would go for months. We wandered like animals. It used to be really difficult to take a moose." Catherine's husband, Steven, spoke as he cleaned his rifle next to the fire.

At the end of the day we tied our boat up to the bank and pitched camp. This was my second year of moose hunting with this family. We sat next to the fire, our cheeks flushed and our stomachs full of black bear meat. Tired from the day's journey down the river, the children were asleep in the tent. The river disappeared into the night, and all that could be seen was the silhouette of conifers along the opposite bank. This land was the home of the boreal Indians.

The ancestors of the Athapaskan Indians are thought to have crossed the Bering Strait from northern Asia to Alaska approximately ten thousand years ago. These northern Indians are probably the least known of American Indian people. Athapaskan territory ranges from interior Alaska

Villagers dancing at a potlatch.

into the Canadian arctic. They pursue their livelihood quietly within the vast reaches of the boreal forest. We know little of Athapaskan history before their contact with nineteenth-century fur traders. Their culture of wood and furs has decayed with the moss over the passing years, becoming buried in the forest which nourished it. Villages which must have existed at one time along the river have vanished with the current which ceaselessly erodes the banks.

A deep relationship exists between the moose and the Athapaskan Indian. The meat that is taken from the giant animal provides food during the long winter. Clothes made from moose hide protect man from the winter cold. Before contact with so-called modernization, a variety of tools and ornaments were made from the bones and the lining of the stomach and other organs. In those days, the capture of a moose must have represented an even greater joy than it does today.

With modernization, the culture of the boreal Indians has undergone great changes. Shamanism has been replaced by Christianity. The American educational system and a materialistic culture have infiltrated this region. However, if you look just below the surface, you will see the hunting culture of a boreal people. In the summer, they take salmon; in the autumn, moose; and in the winter, they capture hibernating bear. From winter through spring small mammals are taken along trap lines.

The curtain of night descends, and the stars grow brighter. It becomes a bit colder, and Catherine continues to speak as she prepares tea.

"When I was little I would go to gather blueberries with my grandmother. I got tired of picking the berries one by one, so I broke off an entire branch laden with berries and took it over to my grandmother. I still remember what she said to me then. 'You musn't break off the branches. Blueberries will no longer grow there, and your luck will turn bad.'"

Catherine's father was the last shaman in this region. He had a great influence on her way of thinking and the conduct of her life. I perceived that despite the change in times and the rapid

Catherine and Steven build a fire in the autumn forest.

influx of new values, Catherine and Steven seemed to be part of an older world. It was a world in which luck and taboos explained everyday occurrences and governed one's actions. Nature's laws were obeyed by observing various taboos. Failure to observe these taboos would result in the loss of one's luck. This sort of consciousness surfaced in the hunting practices that supported the Athapaskan boreal existence. I felt this was a world that must inevitably vanish, however, under the onslaught of modernization.

"Quiet!" said Steven in a loud whisper. "It's a moose!"

We could hear faintly the sound of twigs breaking from within the forest. After a bit we could no longer hear anything. The silence was broken only by the crackling of the fire. We strained our ears to hear more.

"Our luck is good. We'll take a moose tomorrow," whispered Catherine.

Our shelter consisted of nothing but a canvas sheet attached to several trees. The spruce boughs we had spread over the ground felt good under my

back as I crawled into my sleeping bag. I heard the low, clouded hoot of an owl from somewhere in the forest. A young Indian friend had once told me that the call of an owl at night spoke of promises for the hunt to follow. What a fine trip this was. I loved time spent in this way. Thinking that the moose must still be nearby, I strained my ears. The fire went out, and our camp was enclosed by darkness.

I thought about the stories I had heard from Catherine, who lay sleeping next to me. The spirits that reside in all things. Taboos. Luck that surpasses human strength. A world we could not perceive with our eyes. The sound of a moose breaking twigs in the night. The low call of an owl. I could not see either the moose or the owl, but certainly they existed out there in the darkness. Precisely because I could not see them, they seemed to become transformed into something else, another type of existence which was speaking to me of many things. These calls from the night seemed to communicate directly something of the obscure mystery of life itself.

The next morning a moose was standing in the

thickets just downstream from our camp. He gazed intently in our direction, as if he had been awaiting our arrival. A gift from nature to the hunter.

Alces alces gigas . . . the Alaskan moose, the largest deer in the world, crossed over to Alaska from northern Asia in the Pleistocene. The moose pursues a quiet existence in the boreal forest. There is little sound in its movement. Considering the size of the animal, this strikes one as strange. Walking through the forest, I would suddenly become aware of a moose standing right before my eyes. I wonder how many times this has happened? Just as each living thing acts out its own drama, I sense that the boreal forest, too, is now staging a performance.

August draws to a close. Life's program unfolds precisely, as dictated by natural laws. One day you notice that the mountain slopes are faintly colored. The air, which grows crisper each day, gradually dyes the surface of the earth. The blueberries and cranberries ripen, and together with the dwarf birch and the willows, their leaves turn a flaming red and yellow. This mosaic is a feast of colors staged by the brief boreal autumn.

About the time the sandhill cranes head south in their great V formations, changes begin to take place within the forest as well. I hear a low groaning voice with a steady rhythm. Giant antlers weave their way through the spruce trees. The ambling gait of summer has been replaced by a steady walk with a firm purpose.

I hear the sound of antlers butting against trees. The moose has reappeared with a branch of willow dangling from his antlers, the yellow leaves half veiling his face. The eyes that peer through these leaves are not the gentle eyes of summer. In half a day he rubs the velvet from his antlers. It dangles down in so many strips. The moose has entered the rutting season.

The green leaves of summer are gone, and the bull now browses on his winter food of branches and bark. This change of diet, together with hormonal changes associated with rutting, markedly decreases the animal's appetite. Willow shrubs no longer sustain his appetite, but serve as surrogate opponents against which the bull may test his full-grown antlers. It is as if he is sharpening a weapon for battle.

One day the bull moose is attracted by a scent carried on the wind. When he makes his way through the forest, crosses the river, and reenters the forest, he finds a cow moose. The scent is that of the urine of the cow moose, which contains special hormones. He urinates at the same spot himself and stamps the ground with his front hooves as if to stir up the dirt. This is behavior peculiar to the breeding season. Soon the bull catches another scent in the air and is again lured off. In this boreal forest, the moose now lives in a world of scents.

It was at this time that I came across a group of about ten cow moose. A single bull stood among them, as if ready for battle. The fat he had accumulated over the summer armored and transfigured him into a glistening, masculine presence. In rut the bull moose no longer browsed. Mating became his single goal, and he stood ready to challenge any other bull invading his territory. The moose had become transformed into a different animal, driven solely by his mating instinct.

In late September I was witness to a fierce battle. There had been a number of snowfalls, and winter was drawing near. I heard the sound of antlers clashing in the forest. When I approached the spot, the battle was at its height. Two huge bull moose were panting heavily, their antlers locked. The white mist which had formed in front of their faces must have been the result of this labored breathing. The strength of these two bulls hung in a delicate balance as antlers rasped against each other, and snow whirled up at each slight movement.

The moose were indifferent to my presence. At this moment they existed in another world. Suddenly the balance of power crumbled, and one bull charged with a great show of force. The defeated bull stumbled and fled, then suddenly turned about and came charging back at its opponent, locking antlers. KAAAN . . . . That dry sound echoed from mountain to mountain.

The rutting season entered its final stage. On clear nights the aurora danced through the sky, and winter seemed ever closer. My many years in the field had never provided me the opportunity to observe the moment of mating.

That day a change came over the group of moose. Voices of bull and cow moose became more and more frequent. At last the bull entered a stand of spruce, as if to attract a single cow. The long-awaited moment seemed to be drawing near. This warrior, who had driven off all invading bulls and was himself driven by instinct, was now about to perform his ultimate role. The two moose stopped moving, and the bull rested his head on the cow's back. After remaining in this position for some time, the bull suddenly stood up on his hind legs. It seemed that, for a second, his mammoth body hung in mid air. Steadying my breath, I released the shutter as if saying a prayer.

In October the end of the breeding season signals the start of the long, dark winter. The bull moose returns to a solitary existence. These bulls, having lost 20 percent of their weight during the rutting season, must face the winter in a considerably weakened condition. Some, with battle injuries, may face a slow death. Others may meet death quickly at the hands of the wolf, who must also survive the winter.

The forest is again enveloped in silence, as if nothing has happened. Snow falls and covers the trees. The young willows and dwarf birches bend under the weight of the snow, offering soft tips of branches to the moose. Sometimes a moose will rise up on its hind legs and knock down an even larger branch from the dwarf birch. The soft twigs and bark at the tip are now also available to the snowshoe hare who shares this forest.

PAAAN! . . . One cold morning a sound like a rifle shot echoes through the forest. It is fifty degrees below zero. In the extreme cold the trunk of an aspen has split open. Everything on the earth's surface has frozen.

The snow protects small animals from the winter cold, providing an insulating blanket. In December, the moose drop their huge antlers. One winter day a snowshoe hare will find them in the snow. For the small animals, who must pass through the cold northern winters with little to eat, the moose antlers provide a valuable source of calcium. In this boreal forest the circles of life interlock. Under the curtain of the aurora, a fetal moose passes through the same winter.

April. One can feel through one's whole body the days growing rapidly longer. Although the mountains are still covered with snow, there is no longer that tension in the air so characteristic of winter. The night sky is now too light to perceive the aurora, and the season of white nights draws near. As one walks through the forest, the sound of snow falling from spruce branches also speaks of the end of winter.

The surface of the snow, which melts in the warmth of the sun, freezes again in the night cold. As this process is repeated a hard crust forms, greatly impeding the activity of moose. The legs of the moose are cut by the sharp crust as they break through the surface of the snow, and spots of blood may be left behind in their footprints.

When night temperatures at last begin to rise, the snow begins to soften rapidly. Buds swell on the willows and dwarf birch, and moose busily nibble at this early spring feast. The fresh vegetation they have not eaten during the long winter upsets the balance of stomach microorganisms, and it is also at this time that one can see moose undergo a fit of coughing each time they ruminate.

The newly budding antlers of the bull moose are now longer than his ears and are covered by soft velvet. The antlers, which will continue to grow until August, are still very tender, and the bull moose take care not to hit branches with their antlers as they walk through the forest.

In the midst of May winds, a new moose life is born. One day you may run into a cow moose with two calves, but you must not approach them. A cow with calves is very tense. Moving her large ears about like antennae, the cow does not let the faintest forest sound escape her. This new life may become the target of wolves, or of the hungry grizzly who has just awakened from winter sleep.

One day in June I witnessed an unforgettable scene. As I was walking through the fresh mountain greenery, a grizzly pursuing a cow and calf entered my field of vision. The cow and calf were fleeing frantically through a ravine, with the grizzly close behind. As if she thought she could run no longer, the cow suddenly stopped, turned, and charged her pursuer. It seemed like the valiant

Hunting moose along an arctic river.

final act of any weak creature which finds itself defeated. Shrinking back from the charging moose, the bear began to flee. But the cow moose did not give up. The two of them crossed the river and ran up the mountain. Toward the top the cow seemed to be satisfied at last. In the meantime, the calf had kept running, perhaps out of fear, and eventually took shelter in a thicket. To my surprise, when the cow moose returned, she couldn't locate her calf. To my further amazement, she began running about in circles as if she had taken leave of her senses.

Then the mother moose did something quite unbelievable. Once again she crossed the river and began charging up the mountain in the direction of the grizzly. At a distance only visible through binoculars, the moose caught up with the bear. If I were to interpret this action, I would say that she wanted to reconfirm that the grizzly had not taken her missing calf. The relationship between predator and prey seemed to be reversed. Just what is this bond that exists between mother and child, I wondered. The cow moose again descended the

mountain and disappeared in the opposite direction from that of the thicket in which her calf was hiding. I do not know whether this cow and calf were ever reunited.

During the summer season, willow is the primary food source for moose. Shaking its long face back and forth, the huge animal makes its way through the thickets, munching leaves and branches as it goes. Then it ruminates. As these two actions are repeated, summer progresses. After mid-July water plants emerge from the lake bottoms. It is during this time that you can hear water pouring off the moose's face as it lifts its head up into the quiet morning air.

For the growing calf, everything represents a new world: the smell of flowers, the rustling of aspen leaves in the wind, the warning calls of the red squirrel echoing through the forest, and the taste of its mother's milk. To the calf moose, even its own moving body must seem strange. Prancing up, dashing about, bouncing off of things it runs into, the calf explores its world.

In August the bull moose has a set of fully grown

Drying moose meat. Every part of the animal is used, including the organs.

antlers. And, once again, the season of that tremendous instinctive drive approaches.

The potlatch was over and people had resumed their daily activities. Moose-hunting season, too, had passed, and winter drew near.

One day, Catherine and Steven said that they were going to the forest to return the hide from the moose's head.

"Why are you going to do this?" I asked, walking along with them. The world seemed to be dyed a dazzling yellow, as light poured down between the clouds onto the yellow leaves.

"This is what we always do. Because this is what we have always done," replied Steven.

"You have to return the skin from the head to the forest. If you don't, your luck will turn bad," Catherine continued. The cool air of late autumn felt good, and we could smell the scent of the forest.

The covenants that govern man's actions in the natural world — to whom or what, exactly, are these promises made? A moose is taken, eaten, and today a portion of it is returned to nature. This means that the spirit of the moose is returned to the forest.

Now that this has been done, a moose may appear to the hunters once again.

When we emerged from the forest, we came to the edge of a cliff. This was where I had come last year with Catherine's family to gather cranberries.

"There aren't many today, are there?"

The crimson cranberries, which had covered the ground last year, were only evident in patches today.

Be that as it may, what a wonderful sense of space! Lakes and marshes dotted the landscape as far as the eye could see. Oxbow lakes told of the changing course of the river as it slowly carved the landscape through the long reaches of time. Look though we would, we could not see any moose. From somewhere above we heard the high melodic call of the raven.

When Steven and Catherine hung the hide from an aspen branch, I recalled an Eskimo whale hunt in which I had once participated. When they had finished butchering the whale, the Eskimos pushed its giant jawbone back into the sea. As it slipped off the ice pack, the people called out for it

The aurora dances through the long, dark arctic winter.

to return again next year. To return the jawbone of the whale to the sea, to return the hide of the moose head to the forest, is to assure that the circle will not be broken.

In the world inherited by Steven and Catherine, the animals, the trees, the forest, even the wind, all possess spirits and all are attentive to the actions of man. When I am in the boreal forest, my friends' words speak a truth that transcends the realm of myth. There is evident in these northern people an aura of fear, awe, and especially respect for the natural world that is their home. It is a fragile ethic sadly missing in the more developed world. Will it be shattered here as well?

With the twilight came a chill wind. On our way home through the forest we encountered fresh moose tracks. Newly fallen aspen leaves covered the ground, and the moose tracks vanished beneath them.

Michio Hoshino

Above: Every year the bull moose drops his antlers.

Above and opposite: In autumn firm antlers emerge from their velvet sheath.

Above and opposite: As if preparing for the battles of the rutting season, the bull moose tests his antlers against willows and spruce.

Above: Antlers that have just shed their velvet are tinged red with blood.

Moose usually give birth to twins, but it is rare for both calves to survive until autumn.

Following pages: Cow moose "boxing." As they approach estrus, the cows grow tense, breaking out into occasional skirmishes.

The bull wards off an intruder, protecting his breeding territory.

Pages 40–43: A bull's antlers become his weapons during rutting season.

Opposite: A bull moose appears from the forest, offering a challenge.

Above and pages 46–47: The size of the antlers is a symbol of power. When bulls are evenly matched a battle ensues.

Above: Snow swirls up in the air as the animals clash.

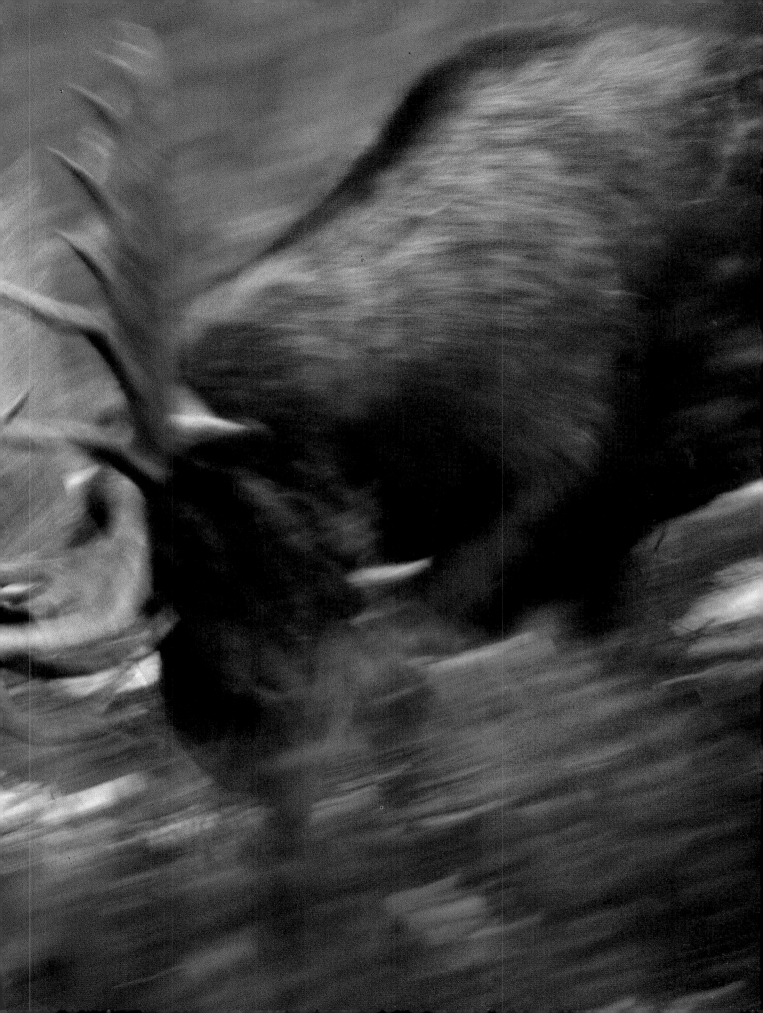

Dawn at Wonder Lake at the foot of Denali. The sound of water pouring off
a moose's head as it feeds on aquatic plants can be heard over the quiet lake.

Following pages: This is a type of mating behavior called wallowing. The cows stop browsing, attracted to the powerful scent of the urinating bull.

Above: The bull is attracted to the scent of the cows and approaches them slowly
through the morning mist.

This page: The cows seem to compete with each other to wallow in the spot where the bull urinates. This behavior may bind the cows to the bull by scent.

Above: The bull entices a single cow, and they enter a stand of trees.

Above: The bull approaches her slowly from behind as if to check her readiness.

Above: In October the rutting season is over and moose return to a solitary existence.
The bull has not eaten for a month and must now face the winter weakened by weight loss.

Above and following pages: In early spring a young moose runs through the valley along a river of snow melt.

Above: Antlers have begun to grow on a bull moose.

Above: A cow with calves is constantly alert for signs of danger in the forest.

Above: A moose swims through the lake in search of water plants.

Above: Because its legs are so long, the calf cannot eat vegetation along the ground without kneeling down.

This page: A grizzly sow and her cub feed on a freshly killed moose calf. If a calf survives the first few weeks after birth, it has a good chance of growing to maturity.

Above: Suddenly a calf ran from the forest and dove into the river. A grizzly chased after it. The two swam against the current frantically.

Above: When the calf was about to dive into the river again, its mother came running to thrust herself between the calf and the bear.

Above: Somehow the calf pulled itself back up on the same bank and mustered its last bit of energy as it ran off.

Above: Tense seconds passed as the two stared at each other intently. The grizzly gave up the prey, and the cow and the calf ran off.

Above: The rutting season again approaches.